Quantum Computing Made Simple

SADANAND PUJARI

Published by SADANAND PUJARI, 2023.

Table of Contents

Copyright

Quantum Computing Made Simple

First Edition: Dec 2023

Book Design by **SADANAND PUJARI**

About

Quantum computing is the most modern field in programming. Is it difficult to study this science? It depends on how the knowledge is presented. In this Book you will study quantum computing the quickest and simplest way.

Don't worry if you don't have enough knowledge of math, like linear algebra or complex numbers. This Book will explain everything you need, so that quantum computing will be as simple for you as school arithmetic.

Also you will understand necessary basics from quantum physics needed for creating quantum algorithms. You will learn what a qubit and superposition are, and get acquainted with the concept of measurement.

Not only will you learn about such amazing things as superposition and quantum entanglement, but you will understand what physical laws govern it, and you will also learn how to use the mathematical tools that can easily describe these complex processes. But most importantly, you will learn how to apply these phenomena of quantum physics in programming. Taking this Book, you will first understand how to move from quantum physics to mathematics, and then from mathematics to programming.

Becoming a quantum programmer is a long road, but the main thing is to take the first step. Let this Book be your first step!

Introduction

Hello, guys, and welcome back to another of my classes. Before we even start, I'd like to thank you all for joining me, cause I'm really happy and would be really, really glad to be your instructor for the next few hours and teach you about the subject of quantum computing.

So before we even start, I'd like to simply tell you that I'm not an engineer in this field, but I'm a programmer and I know a lot of things in this field. So basically what I did is I created a Book about all the basics of quantum computing. So you guys can have a complete introduction about this topic and what we're going to talk about many, many things.

And you'll see by the end of this Book, you have a brief understanding of what exactly this is. So let's start. All right. So basically, what exactly is the goal of this quest? So my first goal right here is teaching you the basics of quantum computing. So here we're going to talk exactly what we're going to talk. What exactly is quantum computing?

We're going to learn all the concepts about quantum computing. We're going to talk about classic computers versus quantum computers. What's the main difference? So I'll try to go as in-depth as possible to help you guys really understand all this topic and at the same time simply understand where exactly the, you know, the world is going and what is the potential of quantum computing in general. Then we're also going to talk about different mathematical concepts.

So basically, the goal of this Book is really teaching you all those concepts. Once again, my goal is not that you guys become professional in those concepts, but simply that you understand them. So basically, we're going to talk about different concepts, such as, for example, complex numbers, which is a concept which is a really important concept in quantum computing.

Not only this, we're also going to talk about one of the basic things. But once again, this is a really basic concept in quantum computing. And you'll see it's going to be pretty cool. We're also going to talk about different algorithms. So basically in quantum computing, in quantum computing, there are plenty of algorithms that exist. Once again, you will not become a professional after understanding them, because while they're a bit complicated, we're going to talk about them and you'll see they're pretty interesting and we're going to learn the logic behind those algorithms.

And so, yeah, I'll try to really give you the simplest one so you will be able to understand them and basically understand all the logic behind all this. And finally, we also are going to write some code, which is pretty cool. We are going with Python to write down codes and we are going to use a tool called Microsoft Cue. Basically, we are going to do this at the end of the Book. Once again, this is not a programming Book, but there is a part of the Book that is strictly for programming.

So basically we are going to learn some basic commands that are with Microsoft. So I'm pretty sure you will like it as well. All right. So what is the Book content? So at first we are going well right now, that's the introduction. So basically in the introduction, we are going to talk about what exactly is quantum computing. So I'm going to explain to you guys what exactly it is, how it works and everything. Also going to talk about all the correct characteristics of a computing system. So basically everything that is around all this. So this way you have a good introduction about this topic. Then we are going to talk about mathematics. So basically the mathematical path, we are going to talk about the concept of Cubitt.

So basically what's a cubit versus what's a bit how everything works and some mathematics around this. We're going to talk about vectors. So basically vectors in quantum computing. We are going to talk about linear algebra, which is pretty important to understand how it works. And we are also going to talk about different things, about complex numbers. What exactly is this topic? What exactly is the concept of complex numbers and everything that we know? Well, we have to know about it to be able to understand quantum computing. Once again, I'm not trying to create professionals. Would you?

Because if I wanted to give a complete class, it's going to take at least nine hours. Well, just to give you a bigger introduction once again here, it's just to show you well, exactly how it works. But just with an introduction, with a basic basic introduction. And finally, we're going to compare a class of computers with their quantum computers. So mathematically, once again, we're going to make some basic operations to help you guys understand what is the difference between those two. Then we're going to talk about different algorithms. So basically different quantum computing algorithms exist.

Once again, I'm going to give you an introduction about all the different types of quantum. Quantum computing algorithms that exist and we are going to talk about them a little bit in depth. So basically the different quantum computing algorithms, you will see how it works. So have a complete part of the Book where we are talking about this. So one example would be, for example, the tour's quantum computing algorithm, which is one of them. Another one could be the Simons, for example. But you'll see we're going to talk about them in this part of the Book. You're going to like it.

And finally, the last thing that we are going to talk about would be an introduction to Microsoft Cube, which is a tool that is used with, well, with Python to be able to perform tasks with quantum computing. Once again, we are doing those tasks on your computer. So we are not using a real quantum computer. But the goal here is really to learn how to write down different algorithms, different quantum computing algorithms on your platform, on your Python app. So basically on your Python text editor in Python with the Python language, for example, in this case with the Python programming language and using Microsoft to do so, basically you will have access to more commands. And those commands are linked with quantum computing.

Once again, we're going to talk about this when we are going to be at this part of the Book. So, once again, my goal here, I repeat, once again, with all those concepts, you will have a really strong knowledge about what exactly is quantum computing. But once again, you will have to practice and take a little bit more to become really a professional in this field.

But you will have a good understanding of disBook about what exactly is quantum computing. All right.

So what you will be able to do by the end of the score. So basically you will understand all the logic, all the logic and basics of quantum computing. So basically, you understand all the basics, all the basic concepts of quantum computing. What exactly is it? Is it everything that is around quantum computing and how all this works? Basically how a quantum computer works. What is the logic behind, for example, a cubit? So basically, what's the difference between a bet and a cubit? I understand how calculations and quantum computing works and why is it more efficient on the quantum computer versus on a normal computer or a classic computer?

We can say it like this. You will have a basic knowledge of math and different quantum computing algorithms. So basically you will have more math knowledge. In this case. We are going to talk about linear algebra. We're going to talk about complex numbers. We're going to talk about plenty of stuff. Once again, I'm not going to give too much in depth in those things, because once again, for each class that I'm teaching you here in, let's say, ten minutes, I can make it a complete five hours class about this topic. So once again, my goal here is really to give you an introduction about each of those topics to help you guys have a better understanding of the concept of quantum computing. Finally, you have some basic knowledge in programming. So once again, I'm not going to give you a python Book right here, but my goal is really to give you an introduction to Microsoft.

Q Basically, the two that we are going to use with the python. So basically we are going to program in Python using Microsoft. Cute. You see, the lines of code that we are going to write will be basic commands. But once again, you'll see it's pretty cool because we are going to use some quantum computing, let's say lines of code, if you want to call it this way, to execute barcodes. Basically, this will give you another introduction to quantum computing and you'll see it's going to be pretty cool to do. All right.

So basically, I hope you guys understand this Schaus well. So until now, my goal is really to give you an introduction to everything. So once again, thanks a lot for joining this class and I'm really happy to be your teacher and help you learn more about this topic. So besides that, let's not waste anymore and let's jump right into our learning.

What Is Quantum Computing

And welcome back to another class of our Book about the complete introduction to quantum computers. So in today's class, we are going to talk more in-depth about the subject and basically understand what exactly is quantum computing. So by the end of the class, you will be able to understand in general what exactly is quantum computing? What's the main difference between classical computers and quantum computers as well? And what areas are they really useful?

And finally, do they exist or not yet? So don't wait anymore and let's jump right into it. All right. So the first question that everybody's asking itself is, what exactly is quantum computing and how exactly do they work? So basically, quantum computers are. Well, the main definition of what exactly this is, will be that quantum computers are an area of computing that is focused on developing computer technologies based on the principle of quantum theories. So when we say quantum theories, we can tell we can think about different algorithms.

We can think about different theories around quantum physics as well as quantum mechanics, which explain the behavior of energy and material on the atomic and subatomic level. So it's really more advanced than basic computation. And so the next thing would be, um, what is the difference between those computers and normal computers? Or basically classical computers will work with ones and zeros. So basically with bits.

But in quantum computing, it's a bit more different because you guys work with Cubitt. So basically, what's the difference between a bit and a cube? It's a bit could be one for zero, but a cubit is a bit more advanced. Well, it could be both at the same time because of the propriety of superposition. Once again, this is a property of quantum computing and we're got to talk about it a bit later. Well, in another class, but just for you guys, just for your information and for you to know that the superposition is one of the properties of quantum computing. So basically, this is a completely different kind of computing, because right now, with operations that can take years to a normal or classic computer to resolve and quantum computing, it can be resolved in seconds. So basically what I'm saying is that it's a different kind of computing.

It is really a different kind of computing because, as I said, classical computers, well, they manipulate ones and zeros and well, because of the power of the cube or not the power of the humans, but basically because of what cubits can bring to quantum computing. This allows us to basically make operations well, do operations way faster than in classical computing and classical computing. All right.

Next thing that we are going to talk about today will be how quantum computing works. All right. So basically, quantum computers or quantum computing works, as I said, with Kupets. So basically, what quantum bits or Kupets? Because Kupets means quantum bits. So basically it works with bits, but they're just quantum. So as I said, those can be one and zero at the same time because of the probability of superposition. And this would give the quantum computer it well, a higher power at work if we compare it to a classical computer.

So in other words, before we can verify if the cubit is a one or a zero, the element can exist in a quantum super superposition. That means you will have the probability of the human being being zero in one. And it's possible to calculate this properly using mathematical formulas basically well, to be able to verify if it's easy or not. So to give you an example, let's imagine that we have two bytes or two bits. So basically the two bits, as I said, could be zero or one. So what can happen? So you have four possible operations that can appear with those two bits.

And basically the operations would be zero zero zero one one zero or one one. So basically, what if we say that each of those bits is and so basically it's an end value. This means that our computer is able to work with values at the same time. So basically with two values in the case that we have two bits, so each bit is one. And so it can work with and it could work just with two values. But if we do the same operation with a cubit, in this case it's a bit more different because each beer, each beer of, let's say, bits together will be considered as a let's say, an element and basically how it will be calculated.

It's going to be a bit more different. So basically because of the probability of. Position, it's possible to well, to have one of the four operations, in other words, two cubits contain two at the power of two artists, four numbers and an cubits will continue to add the power of numbers when a classical computer only contains a number or a number or a number of bits. So basically, if, for example, we have three bids, so basically in a classical computer, we have three bids with three cubits, it's possible to perform eight operations because we have two and it's going to be at the power of three. So basically, as you can see, it grows exponentially.

And because of this exponential growth, it's possible to have way more, more power inside of a quantum computer if you compare it to a classical computer. But it's important also to understand that they're not necessarily better than classical computers. They're just way more powerful in some really specific tasks. So basically, if we have some really specific calculations that we want to perform in today's world, well, they will be basically used for those operations. But we're not yet at an era where we can use it in our everyday life.

So basically, it's really for some specific calculations that are really, really well, it's really, really specialized in those applications and those applications. So basically, if quantum computing becomes a bit more popular and we develop really a lot of quantum computers in what field, they will be really useful so they can be useful in plenty of fields. But four of the more important, in my opinion, are those right here. So the first one will be cryptography.

So everything that is around security and all those things, let's say, for example, we want to perform a brute force attack, well, this is in hacking, so we want to perform a brute force attack on a password. What does this mean? It simply means that we will test all the possible combinations of a certain password. Let's say it's a password that has two characters. So basically there are 99 possible combinations if we only have numbers inside of this password. So if well, with a normal computer, this type of operation will take, let's say, a few seconds.

Now, let's say instead of two elements, we have three elements and there are numbers. So once again, right now, we'll have almost 1000 different combinations. So once again, it's going to take more time to use our classical computer. But let's say, for example, we have 20 numbers inside of our password and there are not only numbers, but also letters and special characters. Well, in this case, it's going to take hundreds of years for our computer, our classical computer, to be able to crack down the password in question. And basically, this is not efficient with quantum computing.

Well, if you guys want to perform this type of attack, it's going to take seconds so it can work this way. But if we reverse engineer, it's possible also to find combinations that will work against all this. So basically to make systems way more secure, to create, as I said, a wee more well, a, we have more important security around, let's say, bank accounts around, credit cards around plenty of things, because once again, with the power of quantum computing, it's possible to do so. It can be really useful for artificial intelligence because once again, artificial intelligence, it's a huge part of the future.

And once again, artificial intelligence requires a lot of calculations. So it could be hundreds of thousands of calculations per second. Well, depending on how advanced we want it to be or how advanced or artificial intelligence to be and basically to be able to perform all those calculations at the same time. Yes, it could work with a classical computer, but it will require a lot of computing power. And if you don't have a lot of computing power, well, the thing is, it's not going to take seconds. It's going to take minutes and even hours with quantum computers.

It's possible to perform all those operations in a fraction of a second. So basically, everything will become way faster, especially in the field of artificial intelligence. When I'm talking, the next thing would be finance. I'm talking about finances right now. It could be, for example, trading. So in the training industry, there is well, there are a lot of people who are performing technical trades. So basically they are working not only with the well, not only with the systems that were indicators in this type of thing, but really more advanced mathematical training. So really based on different algorithms, really based on.

Different mathematical concepts, and sometimes it's not really easy to create a strategy and to back-test it on, let's say, twenty or twenty five years on a second graph. So it requires a lot of calculations. So with quantum computing, it will be possible to test really advanced strategies while more advanced strategies that we have right now and really create a revolution in the financial industry because of a new type of trading that has, well, that way more calculations. And with quantum computing power, it's going to be well, it's going to be a revolution. So basically, because of this, the first companies that will have access to those computers will be able to basically well, we'll be able to make a lot of profits from those computers.

But once again, as I said, they can really be useful for some really specialized desks. So it's not because you're having those computers that you will be able to become a successful trader or succeed in the trading industry. But really, because you have great engineers behind it and well, they develop the strategies. And because of all this, they are able to really, well create great trades with the will, with this quantum computer. So these are some examples of where exactly quantum computing could be really interesting in particle physics as well. But I'm not going to talk too much in depth about this subject. All right.

So finally, do quantum computers currently exist? So this is a great question. So quantum computers are currently well, they are not existing as we think. So basically, they're not small computers that we can have at home and basically work with them. But in October, well, between October of 2000, 2019, Google was able to perform a calculation. Basically, they worked with the department well, they had a partnership with the Naza and basically they were able to perform a calculation.

It really, really advanced quantum calculation that usually would take ten thousand years to a normal computer. But with a quantum computer, they were able to perform this calculation in seconds. So as you can see, the difference between the two is really, really enormous. And this is why quantum computers, in my opinion, are really the future of computing well, especially for those really specialized tasks. So right now, guys, you have a little introduction to the subject. So as you can see, the subject is not simple to understand. But once again, this is a really, really interesting subject and it's really worth it to have an introduction to it. So it's a first class guys and in our next class.

Characteristics Of A Computational System

Hello and welcome back to another class of our Book about the complete introduction to quantum computing. So this is our third class of our amazing Book about this topic. And we are going to talk about different properties and characteristics of quantum computing. So as you'll see in the next few chapters, there are three principal properties that we are going to talk about in this class. So, first of all, we're going to cover superposition. Then we are going to talk about entanglement. And finally, we are going to talk about interference, which are really important properties of quantum computing.

So once again, I'm not going to go too much in depth, but I'll try to start to be as straight to the point as possible. So you guys understand the big picture of those properties. So let's not wait anymore and let's jump right into it. All right. So the first element that we are going to talk about today would be the superposition. So that's the first property that is really important in quantum computing. So basically, when we are talking about superposition and what we need to understand is that this concept is not like gravity.

Well, gravity, that means it can't necessarily be proved. So, yes, we can see gravity, but once again, it can be proved with different laws. Indeed, this concept means that the particle can exist, symmetries similar to and usually in two or more states and that two states can be at the same time. So basically two or more states and at the same time. In other words, basically, if we take a cubit as an example, it will exist as zero or one. So as I said, it's the same thing as a bit, but it means it's a superposition of two states because it will not only exist as zero or one, it will exist as both of them. So in other words, to understand this.

When it's observed, it has only one value, but when it's not observed, it could be zero or one. So basically it's in both states. But the second that we observed the Cubitt, it would be zero or one. But not only this concept exists in quantum computing. We can also find its true nature. So basically it's in nature as well. We can, for example, talk here about different chemical reactions or molecule formations that happen. So basically it's hard for us to observe because of the quantum well, it's hard for us to observe the quantum superposition because once again, it happens really, really fast.

And so it's a basic, well, technical example or natural example. So let's talk about the molecule, H_2O. So this is a molecule of water that is composed of one or two, one atom of oxygen and two of hydrogen. And basically the oxygen will. Well, we'll share its electrons with the atom of hydrogen once again, this is basic, basic chemistry, but in reality, the shared electrons are the same or at the same place at the same time. What an atom of oxygen and hydrogen. So in other words, it exists at both places. So this could be one example in nature.

So basically the atom of, well, the electrons or the electron of oxygen will exist in the hydrogen, in the hydrogen, as well as in the oxygen at the electron of the electrons that will be left behind when this. Well, when the atoms of oxygen will come in, reaction with atoms of hydrogen. So basically you have two electrons that will be left behind. And those electrons, well, they will be in superposition because, as I said, they will be at two places at the same time. So in summary, if we talk about superposition, it will simply refer to the fact that an element can exist in multiple states or places at the same time. So we think this would be for superposition.

The same concept that we are going to talk about today, will entanglement and basically what exactly is entanglement? So personally, I see how I see it. Well, it's a physical phenomenon that can happen when a group of two or more elements interact well, elements interact or are generated or have the same proximity in space in a way that the quantum state of each element of the group can't have an independent description of the state of the others. So basically, entanglement is one of the main features of quantum computing as well as quantum physics.

And so when we talk about an example of one, well, when we talk about an example of entanglement, what we can talk about will be, for example, the example will be, for example, the well to spinning electrons. So let's say we have, for example, two spinning electrons and one is spinning up and the other is spinning down. So basically, if the two electrons are entangled, this will mean that the probability of one electron spinning up will directly affect the probability of the other electrons spinning down.

In other words, whatever you measure for one electron will give you the opposite measure for the other electron. So basically, if something happens to one electron, what happens to one electron will be in direct correlation of what happens with the other electron. So this is what you guys need to understand around this concept. Finally, the last concept that is really important in quantum computing will be interference. And so how we can see it, it's pretty not, it's not simple. It's a bit complicated, but it's a byproduct of superposition. So basically, in other words, that is what allows us to bias the measurement of a cubit toward a desired state or a set of states.

In other words, it's the ability of two waves passing to each other to mingle physically, to work together, or it's similar to the way that ripples communicate in water with each other. So basically and as an example, what I can do. Well, what I find as an example, it could be an interference pattern of light and dark on a screen that will be illuminated by light from two sources. So basically, once again, this is a basic example of interference. So, yes, those concepts might seem a bit complicated and really general. But don't forget that currently we are at the beginning of quantum computing.

And basically those concepts are what I try to explain as simply as possible. But they are way more complicated than I can explain. And there are huge mathematical concepts behind those three really important concepts. But for now, just understand that those three concepts are pretty important in quantum computing. So they said, first of all, we have a superposition, then we have entanglement and finally we have interference that are really important in this well, in the application of quantum computing and everything that is around this type of computing as well as mechanical physics and everything that is around. So that's a first class guys and see all in our next class.

Understanding Complex Numbers
Part 1

And welcome back to another class of our Book about the complete introduction to quantum computing. So in today's class, our main topic would be about mathematics and we are going to talk about numbers in general. So basically a really important concept in quantum computing as well as in quantum mechanics are complex numbers. And basically you need this concept to be able to understand a little bit more.

Well, in my opinion, you need this concept to understand a little bit more the concept of quantum computing and to understand quantum computing as a whole. So what we are going to do today is really have a basic introduction to complex numbers. So we will be able to understand what exactly this is, how it works, and basically how you can represent this on a graph. So let's start. All right.

So basically, the first thing that we need to understand is what exactly is a number? Exactly. So he has the most. The majority of you will say a number is one, two, three, four or five. Yes, this is true. But if we take the definition, basically a number will be a mathematical object that is used to count, measure and label. So as you guys start, it could be represented as one, two, three, four, five. Once again, those are natural numbers, but there is more than just natural numbers.

We have natural numbers. We can have negative numbers. That will be, for example, minus one, minus two, minus three, minus four. We have rational numbers that will be a fractional number of fractions and that can be possibly fractional numbers. We have irrational numbers. So in this case, it will be numbers that can be fractionate because, for example, the square root of two or the square root of five. So basically those numbers are irrational numbers we can have infinities, which would be different that well, you have infinities and different types of infinities.

You have transcendental numbers, which could be, for example, E that is two point seven two, etcetera, or P, which is a really popular, transcendent number. Finally, we have another type of numbers, which is complex numbers that will bring us to the point number two. And basically what exactly are complex numbers? So complex numbers to understand them are simply numbers that actually, well, that until now don't really exist. Well, those are not, you can say, imaginary numbers, what we call them imaginary numbers, but for the moment, we can prove their existence.

So basically, let's say the square root of eight would be equal to minus one. So basically, it's not possible to have a square root of something that will look at the two will be equal to minus one. So basically, it's not possible to have a number that will be at power two and give us one, because the square root of, let's say, a certain number will be plus or minus another number. But if we put this number at the power of two, it's not possible. So was my mistake. So let's say, for example, you have eight at the power of two.

So basically, if you put a power of two, even if it's a negative number, it will automatically become a positive number because, for example, let's say we have minus two, eight equals minus two and it's a power of two and basically it will be four. So the answer will always be a positive number. But instead we have, let's say, a at the power of two and it gives us a negative number. Basically, we don't know what eight is. So this would be a complex number because we can't really prove that it exists. What's the difference between all numbers and complex numbers?

As I explained, it's really hard to work with complex numbers because once again, they don't really exist. We expose them hypothetically and you will see in the future graphs how we can represent them well, how we can represent them on the chart. Basically, we have other numbers, well, we can work with them. It will be, for example, one, two, three, four, five. So we can work with rational, irrational numbers, negative positive numbers.

You can work with all types of numbers and basically with complex numbers. It's a bit more complicated, but it's possible. So an example of a number. For example, in this case, we can have five. That is a rational number, minus 20. That will be a negative number. So we have P e that will be, in this case, transcendent numbers. You can have all three and seven five. They can be another type of number. And we have complex numbers. So you can see here we can have an example of complex numbers. So in this case, we can have I at the power of two that will become minus five. So in this case, even if it's I don't know if you can choose the number that you want, if you take any number of the power of two, it can become negative numbers. So basically, this is impossible.

And those will be simply other examples in this case, we have a function and let's say, for example, five is a complex number, so basically it's going to become complex. So you will have one part of this function that will not be complex. So it will be enormous, the rational and normal number that we can work with. So in this case, it's going to be three and in this case it's going to be minus seven. And the five right here will be part of the rational, not rational of the complex number. So how exactly we can put this all on a graph so it's possible to show these types of functions on a graph and basically how exactly this would work.

So let's work with this function right here, which is three plus two. So in this case, if G is the imaginary number or a complex number. So what we'll do is pretty simple. We'll use the X axis as real numbers. So we will put our real numbers right here and G or here will put our Y's. We'll use our Y's as imaginary numbers. So pretty simple. We'll have our function right here, which will be three plus two G. And we want to represent what will have this number right here. Three plus two does not really function and want to represent that on each other. So pretty simple what we'll do.

Simply put, the three right here. So basically we will have our real number, which is three, and that will simply select three right here. And two, since it's a part of our complex number, we'll put it right here. So basically to represent our complex number on a graph. It's going to be like this. So as you can see here, we will have our complex number that is represented this week. But since we don't know what she is, I will simply use the two to be able to represent it. So basically, here we have our Xs, you will have our wise Xs will be real numbers and the ways will be our complex for imaginary numbers.

So as you can see, I explained it right here. So for this number right there, the real number of this operation will be three and the imaginary number will be two. So another type of representation. So basically here you have plenty of the complex numbers that you guys can see. So this operation right here explains that really simply. So we'll have our 8:00 a.m. hour. In this case, a real number and B will become part of the imaginary number access. So in this case, let's see a few examples. So, for example, we have our three. In this case, it's going to be our eight and our two.

I will be our B so easily here. Our imaginary number will be right there. Same thing for if, for example, the number is negative. So it could work for both. For example, if our weight is negative, we will put our number right here. So A negative and B, positive, it's possible. And B, negative, it's possible. Just being negative and eight, positive. It's possible as well. As you can see, this is the way that you guys can represent a complex number on a graph. Once again, pretty hard working with those numbers, but it's possible and this is a really important concept to understand.

Well, to understand for the future classes and simply to understand quantum computing. So as I explained today, we talk about numbers, just to summarize everything. We talked about numbers. We talked about all types of numbers as well as complex numbers, which is really important in this type of computing. So you guys understood everything. So that's a first class guy. And see you all in our next class.

Understanding Complex Numbers Part 2

Hello, guys, and welcome back to our class of our Book with the complete introduction to quantum computing. So in today's class, we are still going to talk about complex numbers and basically their use in quantum computing and simply their use in general. So since this is an introduction and an introduction Book, basically, well, I'm not going to talk about all the mathematical concepts and make all the mathematical proofs, because some of you guys simply don't have the mathematical basis for all this.

So my goal here is really to present to you or present you complex numbers and explain your complex numbers. As for beginners. All right. So basically, we talk about complex numbers and the best class. And what we'll do today is really understand why they're used and what exactly are the properties of those numbers. All right. So basically, complex numbers are used. So there are plenty of fields where we can use complex numbers, but it's not really used in everyday operations.

So let's say, for example, you guys are going to a store, the person who will serve you or even you when you're buying something, you will not use complex numbers to calculate. I don't know how many apples you are going to buy or how much it's going to cost you again. So basically, you will make normal calculations. But complex numbers have utilities in more advanced calculations. And so basically in advanced physics, in advanced mathematics, they're really present and this is where they are. So basically some examples of fields where they are used. Well, it can be used in many fields, such as electricity, for example.

It can be used in mechanics. It could be used in engineering or even in the country in quadratic operations. Well, equations, sorry. And when we're working with a quadratic plain and those numbers will simply be it will simply never touch the x axis. So what does this mean? So let's say, for example, we have a complex number that is equal to five plus I in this case, let's say five plus well are five plus. I will be a complex number.

So basically in this number, the real part will be the five. So basically five is a real number and the complex number will be one multiplied by eight. So in this graph, when you are drawing the graph of five plus I, what you'll see is that the X will be five and Y will be one because basically the white represents all the well, all the imaginary numbers and the X will simply represent the real numbers. So in this case, the X could never be zero. And why? It's pretty simple because if it's equal to zero, our imaginary number will simply not exist because everything that you multiply by zero will be equal to zero.

So basically this will make our complex number disappear and we will only have one real number. So basically, it's not a complex number anymore. So this is why it's never. Well, it's never, it will never have X equal to zero as well as a complex number. And also they are really useful in more advanced calculations. So basically, as I said at the beginning, when you are working with more advanced calculations, especially in physics and all this stuff, they're really useful. So why are complex numbers used in quantum computing, in quantum computing?

So basically the main purpose of using complex numbers, especially in quantum computing, is to make your operations way more simpler. In other words, when you are working on quantum computing, but not only in quantum computing, but in mathematics in general, when you are going to more advanced mathematics or more advanced physics, what's going to happen is that you will have very heavy operations. So you will have really, really, really big operations.

And to be able to work properly with those operations, you need to simplify them. And the best way to simplify those operations is simply to simplify. Very heavy concepts will be the use of complex numbers. And basically those complex numbers help us make those operations way more easier. So an example of something that is really useful, for example, advanced mathematics or advanced mathematics, more the algebra part or advanced physics will be linear algebra. So basically, it's really used in quantum computing.

This part will be heavily simplified with the use of complex numbers because it will allow us to make Haiti operations way smaller and in this case, make them way more easier to work with. So this is why complex numbers could be really useful, especially well in more advanced fields. All right. Now let's talk about the properties of complex numbers. So in this case, complex numbers have three main properties. So they can be commutative, they could be associative and they could be distributed.

So it's not really hard to understand, but I think it's really important to understand it as well. So for the community commutative park, what exactly this means, it's pretty simple. That means that changing the order of the operation will not change the result at the end. So let's say we have the same complex number that we have before us, or a complex number is eight equals to eight plus five. So in this case, I plus five would be our complex number. If instead of it plus five, we have five plus I'm changing.

The order inside of operation will not affect the complex number. And so simply changing. Well, changing the order of one number two in front of another number will leave us with the same complex number at the end. So basically, this is the first really of our properties of complex numbers. The second one will be associated. So basically a complex number is a subsidy, and that means that we can group the terms how we want. It will not change the results. It's pretty good, it looks like the first one. So it's a bit like being commutative, but it's a bit different because instead of working with just one number, instead of changing like one number of places, we are talking about a group of numbers.

So let's say, for example, we have our complex number, which would be eight plus five plus eight plus seven. So right now we have four numbers in the first group which will be eight plus five, and the second group will be eight plus seven. So in this case, changing places plus seven with eight plus five will simply not affect the complex number at the end. So basically, if we write down eight plus seven plus eight plus five, it's the same thing as writing down eight plus five plus eight plus seven.

So this is another property of complex numbers, changing groups while changing terms inside will change in group terms inside of the equation of the complex number will not affect the complex number. And finally, the last part is this: a complex number is distributed. In other words, in multiple ways. Well, what's going to happen is that it respects the propriety of operations. So what we need to understand here is that, for example, multiplication will go over, in addition, for example, where division will go over and over again. So we have our complex.

We have a complex number eight once again, and it's going to be two multiplied by plus five. So let's put it plus five in parenthesis. So what's going to happen is that the branches are respected and the multiplication will be respected as well. So finally, A will be simply equal to two, multiplied by plus two multiplied by five. You can see the property of operations is respected, the practices are respected, and everything is what works perfectly. And all the properties of operations are respected as well.

So to summarize everything we talked about in this class, we simply talked about the properties of complex numbers and where they can be used, what exactly the complex numbers are used for and why they are used in those fields. So, as I said, I will not go too much in depth in this concept because the more

I go in depth, the more it's going to be hard to understand what is for you guys to understand that they exist.

And they are really, really used, especially in quantum physics, quantum computing, as well as in advanced mathematics, in mechanics, physical mechanics, well, quantum mechanics and some other really advanced mathematics fields. So that's all first class guys in our next class.

Mathematics For Quantum Computing Part 1

Hello, guys, and welcome back to another class of, Of course, about the complete introduction to quantum computing. So into this class, we are going to talk about mathematics showing the best new class.

We talked about complex numbers, and today we are going to start the talk about mathematics. So basically we're going to talk about some mathematical concepts that are really used in quantum computing as well as quantum mechanics. So basically, we're going to talk about linear algebra and some concepts of this type of math. So basically, this is algebra.

And what we are going to talk about today will be vectors. So basically the first thing that we need to know is what exactly are vectors? So vectors are pretty well, it's not really hard to understand, but it's a major part of quantum mechanics and it's a huge part in physics and mechanics as well as in quantum computing. So basically, we can see vectors as a list of numbers and there are many ways to interpret what this list of numbers means. So basically, in other words, a vector is a point in space. So you can see right here and the list of numbers that it contains is just a way to identify where the point is in space.

So basically a vector will come in a form of, well, not a matrix, but it will come in a form of two or three numbers. And basically you will be able to draw a two dimensional or a three dimensional vector in space. So what? It will always start from zero and it will go from zero to, let's say, for example, a certain number. So I'll show you some examples a bit later on the graph.

You'll see it's pretty simple to understand, but basically what a vector is. It's simply a line that is drawn in space. So where exactly vectors are used to basically have many, many utilities and they are pretty much everywhere. So, for example, in real life, if we're talking about real life, we can think about all the situations that will involve a certain force or velocity. So let's say, for example, someone is running in the street. So the energy that this person is spending to run in a certain direction can be a vector.

So basically the direction in which this person will run would be a vector that will point to the front. But all the forces, for example, the wind, for example, the inclination and all the other forces that do ensure that the person well can't run as fast as he usually can. In, for example, the treadmill would be a vector in the other direction. So we're seeing the reverse. And basically those two vectors will tell how fast the person will, for example, run. So let's say, for example, this person will run five km.

Well, we'll run from point zero to point five. But there is a resistance from point five to point. Well, there is a resistance from point zero to point minus two, for example, once again. So you will see that this person will run from point zero two point three, for example, because we make an addition of those vectors. So this could be one way that we can use vectors in real life. So basically, if we go a little bit more advanced, we can calculate the speed that this person is running.

We can, for example, know how much time it will take this person to run a certain distance based on multiple variables. For example, as I said, that could be the wind, could be the inclination of where the person is running. It could be the obstacles and the streets could be plenty of things. And the vectors will be integrated into this calculation. All right. The property of vectors, basically, is pretty much the same as for complex numbers. So basically vectors are commutative.

So basically the order of operations doesn't really matter in this case. If, for example, we have vector eight plus vector B, it will be equal to vector B plus vector and finally it's distributed. So basically in this case, it respects the property of operations. So multiplications, for example, where divisions will pass before additions or. So here are some examples of vectors. So basically when we are writing a vector, we will write it inside. So in this case, Barrett's are the little things right here that you can see. And those are well, those are Barretts and this is how we write them.

So basically what we can see right here would be, for example, vectors. So here we root vectors. So as you can see, we can make an addition of vectors. So in this case, it's going to be vector E plus vector will be equal to the. And if we decide to make a multiplication of vectors, it's pretty much possible. So let's say we are multiplying eight by vector eight plus vector B, it will give us A multiplied by vector eight plus eight, multiplied by vector. And as I said, if we want to represent all this inside of each word, so let's say, for example, we have two vectors to Victor.

It will be right here and Victor will be right here. If we make an addition of eight plus B, it will look something like this. So basically we are auditioning Victor eight plus and Victor B, it will give us this answer right here. So this would be vector eight plus B, so this is basically how we create well, how we make an addition of vectors, multiplication a bit more different. But once again, it's all basic linear algebra. It works pretty much the same way as matrix multiplications and additions and all this stuff. So as you can see, well, it's not the middle point between Victor in Victor, but once again, it's possible to add those two vectors together as well, in usually mechanical physics, as well as quantum mechanics and quantum computing.

We are working with something that is a bit more different. So basically, since we're working with complex numbers and those numbers are pretty much imaginary, it's a little bit hard to show those vectors well to be able to show those vectors in a visual representation. So the majority, well, technically, it's hypothetical. Those factors are hypothetical, but it's well, it's complicated to show them visually. That's what I'm trying to say, because if, for example, we have a two dimensional vector, we should use four dimensions to represent the same thing.

If we have a three dimensional vector that we are working with, if we use complex numbers, we will need at least six dimensions. So basically, this is what a well, this is what it will basically look like. So the type of vectors that is used in quantum computing is called Euclidean vectors. And the thing with those vectors is they're really general. So basically, this is why we work with this specific type of vector and those vectors are really once again, generally, we can see it this way. So it's not it's not like vectors that work with real numbers. So it's really specific for imaginary numbers. And it will give us a more general answer to, for example, the vector that we are looking for. And it's really useful for Cubitt. So basically, when we are working with qubits, there is a huge part of quantum computing.

We'll talk about it a little bit later. But you'll see that once again, this is a huge part of quantum computing. Hubert's and vectors are really important in this book. All right. So I hope you guys right now understand the basics of victories and what exactly can do with it. And as I said, this is a really important part in linear algebra, quantum mechanics and quantum computing as well. So he's a first class guy in our next class.

Mathematics For Quantum Computing Part 2

Hello and welcome back to our class of our Book about the complete introduction to quantum computing in today's class. We are still going to talk about mathematics and more precisely, linear algebra. And so my goal today is to present to you three, three really important properties that are in linear algebra that you guys need to understand.

And basically, it's really important if you guys are continuing mathematics or if you continue in quantum computing as well. And basically you will see those properties are pretty simple to understand. I'm not going to make the whole mathematical explanation about each of those. My goal is really to go straight to the point. So you guys understand what exactly is each of those properties. So let's start. All right.

So basically, the first property that we are going to talk about today will be linear combination and what exactly is linear combination? So basically how we can see it, we can see it as the sum of two factors that have been killed by numbers. So in this case, for example, would have a multiplied by vector A plus B multiplied by a vector. So basically, in this case, A will be scaled by the vector eight. So as you can see right here, and this is why those two vectors will be in linear combination, what you can do also.

Well, here I give an example of two vectors, but you can add as many vectors as you want. You can add vectors C, D, E, and et cetera, the number of vectors that you want. Another example that I can give you, for example, would well, for example, be, for example, the linear combination of X and Y. So basically I'd say you have two variables that would be X and Y. So basically what's going to happen? You will have the constant A and let's say, well, you will have a constant and multiply by X plus a constant multiplied by Y, so B, C you will have two constants multiplied by X and Y and you will have a linear combination between X and Y as well. So this would be the first property.

The same thing that we are going to talk about is linear dependence. So basically linear dependence works a little bit with the linear combination and what we can see right here. For example, while linear linear dependence, for example, Vector A, B and C will be linear dependent if some vectors. Well, let's say you have three or four vectors that will be vectors A, B, C, D, they will be linear dependent if some vectors of the group can be expressed as a linear combination of other vectors in this group. So let's say we have three vectors in our case to ABC.

And so in this case, let's say a multiply by victory plus B multiplied by victory, we know that this is a linear combination that will be equal to victory. This would mean that C can be expressed as a linear combination of A and B.. So this would be the first part of the operation and those three industry vectors would be linearly dependent. So basically, if you take the operation or the basic operation right, you will know that the Vector C will be the linear combinations with a combination of those two vectors right here multiplied by constants. And basically this at the end will be, well, this operation right here will do that. The three vectors will be linearly dependent.

Finally, the last element that we are going to talk about will be leaning independents and what exactly is leaning independents, pretty simple. It's simply the reverse of leaning independents. This simply means that there are no winners in the group. They can be expressed as a linear combination of the other factors in the group. So if you guys are a little bit lost with this terminology, well, the last one, it's pretty simple. It's pretty much the reverse of your dependence. So basically, it's well, it's not it's the complete reverse of dependence.

This could be a good way for you guys to understand Leanyer independents. So those are the three properties that we talked about to Maisky. There are really important factors. So we could work with vectors and in mathematics in general. So we talked about linear combination, linear dependence and finally linear independence. I hope you guys understood the basics of those concepts. So that's it for us, because guys, you all know our next class.

Mathematics For Quantum Computing Part 3

And welcome back to a class of our Book about the complete introduction to quantum computing. So in this class, we are still going to talk about the mathematical aspect of quantum computing and we are still staying in linear algebra. So what we are going to cover today will be three basic notions that are pretty important in, well, linear algebra in general and in quantum computing as well.

So basically what we will cover today will be spends, bases and finally dimensions of space vectors. So basically my goal today is not to make all the mathematical demonstrations of each of those elements, but simply to introduce you the most simplified to those notions because they're a little bit complicated. So let's start. All right. So the first thing that we are going to talk about will be a sense basically what exactly is a spin? So it's part of a set of vectors.

We can see it simply as the set of all linear combinations that those vectors have. So, for example, let's say we have two numbers that would be A and B, for example, and that we have two vectors. So those vectors will be vector one and vector too. So this would mean that the spin of vector one and vector two is the set of all vectors of the equation. That will be our number one. So you multiply by vector one plus B, which is our saying number multiplied by vector two for some colors eight and.

Now, what is the difference between the span and a linear combination? So, yes, there is a pretty major difference between those two elements. So what we need to understand in this case is that a linear combination will simply be a sum of scalars multiplied. Well, some of the sculler multipliers of elements that are in one base basic set. The span, it's a bit different. Is a bit different. So since the span of a busy set is the full list of all linear combinations that can be created from the element of that basis, of the basis set multiplied by a set of colors. So what we need to understand is what exactly is the basis. So in linear algebra, basically, well, a basis is how we can see a basis.

We can see what, we can see a basis for a vector. Space V is a linearly independent set that can span that span. So in other words, if V is given as the span of some sets of vectors, then a basis can be obtained by simply throwing out redundant vectors. So this would be for a basis. Finally, the last concept that we need to understand, the word that I wanted to present to you today will be the dimension. And it's really important to, well, not to talk about, but to understand the difference between the dimension of a space vector and the dimension of asymmetry.

So basically, for those of you who understand well, who did the basic linear algebra impact, the dimension of the matrix is simply the number of columns versus the number of rules. So basically it will simply give us the dimensions. So what exactly our metrics will look like. So basically for the dimensions part, let's say we have a vector V for, well, the space vector of this vector, this space vector expanded by an infinite set. So then it is set to be finished in dimensional. And in this case the dimension of the will be the number of vectors in a basis for.

Now let's say we have a vector space zero. So basically in this case it is going to be zero, then the dimension will be defined as zero because our vector space will be zero in this case. So it will look good. It's going to be zero if I leave our vector space. Well, this is for the last type of picture space that we can have that is not sponsored by a finished set. Then it is called an infinite dimensional vector space. So basically there are three types. So it could be finished, it could be defined as zero.

And finally it could be infinite and infinite dimensional vector space. So those were the three elements that I wanted to talk about in this class. My opinion, they're pretty important that they don't. As I said, they don't want to make all the mathematical demonstrations about each of those elements, because once again, it's a bit complicated to understand and even to teach well in words and try to put it as simply as possible. But this is what you guys need to understand from those terminologies. So that's a first class guy in all of our next class.

Mathematics For Quantum Computing Part 4

Hello and welcome back to another class of our Book with the complete introduction to quantum computing. So in today's class, we are still going to talk about mathematics and we are going to talk about linear algebra as well. So basically pretty much the same thing as we talked in the past few classes today. What we are going to talk about is pretty simple.

So we are going to have an introduction to Matrices and I'll show you some operations that you guys can perform with Matrices, basically what it's used for. And we are going to understand basically what is the difference between Matrix's scholars, inspectors and all the stuff. So let's start. All right. So basically, what exactly is a matrix in linear algebra?

So basically a matrix is a rectangular array of numbers, or it can also be symbols that are arranged in rows and columns. So basically, let's say we have a matrix with X rows and why columns. So it's going to be an X multiplied by white matrix. So here you can have an example of what the Matrix is. So basically we have in this case three columns and well, she comes and two. So basically this is an example of the Matrix. You can have way more columns and more rows as well. Another thing is color.

We don't have color right here. So basically color is just a number inside of a row or a column and a vector. So basically a vector can simply be a column or so. In this case, a vector will be six one or you will have a three dimensional vector since we have three numbers. So basically, here we have another victory. So basically six one and we saw in the past few classes how victories well, how victories look like on a graph. So we're exactly metrics are used in real life so they can be used in many fields. Those fields can include, for example, statistics, finances, research or scientific studies.

And as I said, in pretty much any field scientific studies, matrices can also be used to represent the real world data. So when we're talking about real world data, we can, for example, think about the population, the population of lions in Africa, for example, or I don't know, the quantity of pizzas created in a restaurant. So basically anything that can well, anything that uses numbers and statistics and counting basically can be we can work with Matrices there.

Yes, I give you some really basic examples, but basically it's a little bit more advanced, but you can use metrics for those examples as well. So this is what Imageworks is now. What type of operations you guys can perform with Imitrex. So in what a matrix, you can perform well for normal numbers. You can perform four types of operations. You can perform an addition, a division and multiplication and subtraction. When you guys are working with a matrix, with rows and columns, there are three things that you guys can do. So basically the first step of operations will be really switching. So it's when you guys are performing a room switching operation.

I'll show you examples of it later. So when you guys are performing rule switching, it's really important to focus on copying the right numbers. Exactly, because you will have a mistake after that and you can perform in addition to basically auditioning metrics together. But once again, you need to have the same metrics. So basically here you can have an example.

And finally, you can perform eight multiplications in mattresses. So let's start with the first one to basically rule switching looks something like this. So as you can see, what we have done here is pretty simple. So we just took the first group and we put it at the end right here. So basically what we've done, we simply changed the rules. So this is a permission to do when you guys are working with metrics and then you can use these metrics and make an addition of these metrics to other metrics. For example, it's going to be pretty much the same thing. So, as I said, the same type of operations that you guys will perform or you can perform with metrics as will be the addition.

So in this case, we would have an addition right here. So it's pretty simple to understand it. So, as I said, really important, the metric size should be the same. So basically, in this case, the metric size is a two by two. So basically it should be two by two. Now you cannot make an addition of a two by two by three by two. For example, it will not make sense. So here we have a two by two and that you guys can perform an addition. So basically how it will work. So you will add a different number with the first number right here, the second number with the same number and same thing right here. There's no water, no fourth number with the numbers.

So you can see it's pretty simple that the type of operations that you guys can perform will be, in this case, the multiplication. So it's not that it's more complicated. It's not that complicated, it's just you guys need to get used to it. So basically how this would work. So pretty simple. Let's say you have this metric, this metric right here multiplied by this vector right here, since it's two numbers, just one column. So basically, I can see here the way that you guys will perform the operation is pretty simple. You will simply multiply your eight by the X and then you make an addition of the B multiplied by the white right here, then the same thing C multiplied by X plus the multiplied by the white. Right.

So you can see it's well, it's not complicated to perform those operations and for Matrices it can be really, really useful. So basically here we have metrics multiplied by vectors, but it's possible to multiply matrices by other metrics. And as you can see, numbers can grow pretty much. Well, we have metrics multiplied by a vector, but if we have a matrix multiplied by a matrix, you will have more operations to perform. So in this case, quantum computing can be really, really useful when you guys have huge amounts of operations to perform.

So this is for the basics of linear algebra and therefore the basics of metrics is what we talked about, some other things, both linear algebra in the past few Books. But this is really one of the court things. Understand, when we're talking about linear algebra, we have vectors, but right now we have metrics as well and there are a huge part of this set of linear algebra, mathematics, so basically this type of mathematics. So it's at first glance, guys, in our next class.

Mathematics For Quantum Computing Part 5

And welcome back to the class of our Book about the complete introduction to quantum computing. So this class topic, we are still going to talk about linear algebra since we are still talking about mathematics. And my main goal today is to introduce you guys to the concept of projection. So basically, what exactly is a projection in linear algebra? So it's pretty simple to understand.

You'll see maybe the concept seems a little bit complicated, but when you see what it looks like, you'll understand that it is pretty simple. All right. So let's start with what exactly is projection in linear algebra and all its real life applications. So basically, linear algebra, a projection is simply a well, the projection is simply a linear transformation from a vector space to itself. So we can see it, for example, that is, let's say, for example, the vector space.

Well, let's say that the linear projection B will be P2. It will be equal to P. So in other words, whatever P will be applied twice, any value to any value, it will give the same result as if it were applied only once. So it means that it's important. So it leaves its image unchanged. So basically, the projection of a vector space can be a linear operator. So what exactly is the projection of a vector?

So the direct projection is the vector that is produced when one vector is resolved into two component vectors. One is parallel to the second vector and the one that is perpendicular to the second vector, the parallel vector on the vector projection. So in other words, basically you will have two vectors and what it will look like, basically it's going to be one vector will go over the other vector. So it's a bit complicated to see right now because there are no pictures. But in the example part, I'll show you what it looks like. And we are going to talk about the formula behind what a projection is.

And finally, what our new life applications of a projection. And what exactly are projections, Don, if it's just one vector on another vector. So its utilities are mostly in physics or basically in physics and in research. So it can work, for example, for acceleration, displacement, electrics or electric or magnetic fields, gravity, gravitational fields, anything that is with acceleration, deceleration and the movement of objects can use, well, projection of vectors. So basically vector projection works and uses the concept of projection. So there are plenty of well, plenty of ways of using it, but it's mostly used in physics.

So when we were talking about, well, if you want to understand this concept a bit more easily, it's pretty simple. So here you can see a graph. So basically you're going to have to vector. So let's say this is the vector V and this is the vector Y. So basically what we can see here is that there will be a sun and this will be the shadow of the vector. Of the victor. So basically, this is simply the shadow of the victor and it's going to go all over the victor, quite so if this Victor right here is smaller, well, it's going to only partly under Victor White.

And if it's really large, well, it's going to go completely over the victor way. So basically, the concept of projection is simply one victor going over the other one. So, as I said, it's something that is pretty simple. Now, how can we determine what will be the distance of this vector right here? So basically of the projected vector right here. So basically, as you can see, the blue line, well, in this case, it's the green line or the blue and what the projection of this vector is, how exactly we can see what it's at length so that we will find it is pretty simple.

We have this formula right here. So before we start, just to understand the first part of the formula right here. So the division will be in other words, this is just one number. So basically what we'll do will calculate the distance of the vector. We'll multiply by the vector y divided by the vector Y multiplied by the vector white. So basically here will have Y at the power to you will have V multiplied by white and will simply divide this part of the formula by this part of the formula right here. Y will be a vector. So basically it's not a scholar.

So what we'll do will multiply this part of the operation which is a scholar by a vector. And what it's going to give us is going to give us a vector and that basically we will know exactly what will be the length of our new vector. So this is the main goal of this operation. So at the end, we are able to know exactly what will be the length of the vector that is projected inside of our well, inside of this formula. So now you guys have an understanding of what exactly is a projection, another way, for example, that we can use, for example, projection will be simple.

Let's say, for example, we have a mountain, so this would be a mountain and there will be something on this mountain. So basically, let's say, for example, that I don't know, we have the force or the gravity, the gravity gravitational force that will push our object from the mountain. And we need to apply a certain force. So basically we can use projection to be able to understand what force we need to apply. To be able to lift this object, this is going to be a bit more complicated because we need to take into consideration the mass of the object, the speed that the object goes.

And there are some other factors, but basically so in order to understand how we can move this object, we need to understand projections. So basically, projections can be really useful in those cases. So you guys right now understand what exactly is projection. You want your profession, what you want to be a professional about and projections and be able to at least be able to understand what is projection as an introduction to it. So that's at first glance, guys can see all in our next class.

The Concept Of Qubit Part 1

Hello and welcome back to our class of, Of course, about the complete introduction to quantum computing. So into this part of the Book, we are going to talk about. So, yes, I know that at the beginning of this class, we talked about Cubitt and some other aspects, like, for example, superposition and some other things. But in this part of the question, we are going to talk really more mathematically about this.

So, yes, we're going to have a refresher about what exactly it is. But we are going to talk about some other concepts and as I said, the mathematical aspects of this amazing concept. So let's start. All right. So basically how exactly a cubit is created. So this is a little bit more theoretical, but to create a cubit, you need an object that can attain a state of quantum superposition between two states. So, for example, we can think of what an atomic molecule can be, one kind of a cubit. So basically this type of particle can spin and point in different directions in respect of a certain magnet magnetic field. So basically, we have a magnetic field.

We will have this particle that will be here and will spin in different directions. So this could be one type of another, we can be stripping an electron of these atoms. Obviously we are taking an electron from an atom and turning it into an iron. Then with electromagnetic fields, it's possible to spend it in. Well, we will suspend it and it's going to be in free space. And all this thanks to electromagnetic fields. So with the magnets.

Then this would create a trap for an iron quantum computer. So this is a way to create the quantum computer, what?

To create cubits, to be able to create a quantum computer after that. So how accurate is it useful in quantum computing? So basically. A cubit is what quantum computing is, it's the basic unit of quantum information. Well, quantifying information, I mean, so in other words, how we can see it, it's basically like the bit for the normal computer, so. Well, for the classic bit. And they're basically without the Cuban, there is no quantum world, there's no quantum superposition and there are no quantum computers. So this is why this is really useful in quantum. Well, in quantum computing.

And this will bring us to our third point that asks us how it is more powerful than a bit. So basically here, as I said, it's really well equipped. It's really more useful than a bit. Why? It's because it's able to operate more than one operation at a time. So basically a bit will be able to generate only one answer. So basically, if we have two bits, we have two possible answers. If we have two cubits, it's different. We have two powers and possible answers. So basically, if we have ten bits, we'll have ten different answers that are possible. But if we have ten cubits, we can have two powers, ten different answers, which is way more powerful.

And this is exactly where the power is. It offers way more operations and waits less time. So basically operations that can take years to complete with a normal computer can take eight seconds to complete with a quantum computer, maybe minutes. So basically, it allows us to go way, way faster with our technology, basically, and allows us to, well, we make way more operations. And this opens doors to weigh more things. And more new technologies. So what are the fields of utility, so there is not that much field of utility above.

So basically it's really useful in physics. So all the materials that are around the concept of Cubitt are really useful there. They can also be used in mathematics. So basically, once again, talking about the mathematics behind itself is useful in quantum computing. So basically, as I said, this is the main meaning. Well, the main item inside of a quantum computer and basically this is like eBid for a normal computer. So we needed to be able to work with information. Is really useful in this case and this is its main utility. So basically quantum computing could be the main utility, but all the theory behind it.

So basically all the mathematical and physical concepts behind this can be really useful in different fields such as mathematics and physics. So basically, all the fields that are around the computer now, is it possible to build a computer at home? Theoretically, yes, it can be possible if you guys have a lot of money and a lot of knowledge in this field. But in the majority of cases, it's not really possible. It's possible to work with different programs that allow you to create different quantum algorithms such as Microsoft Cube, for example. Well, yeah. So such as IBM has this program, Microsoft has its own program as well.

There are other programs that are being created that you guys can use to be able to work with the quantum algorithms. And once again, it's possible to do this, but to create a computer at home. It takes, as I said, a lot of knowledge and also a lot of money, because once again, those are the things that you guys will use to be able to create this technology costs a lot. So in theory, yes. But in practice, it's really, really hard.

So once again, the source was that this class was really theoretical. And my goal here is really to give you once again an introduction, which is the main benefit of what is the main concept in quantum computing when we are talking about storing information and transferring information, sergeant first class guys and all in our next class.

The Concept Of Qubit Part 2

Hello and welcome back to another class of our Book for the complete introduction to quantum computing. So in today's class, we are still going to talk about the concept of Cubitt. And basically we are going to understand a little bit what exactly this is and all the mathematical aspects of this amazing concept that is inside of quantum computing. So let's start. All right.

So basically, what we are going to talk about today would be working with multiple qubits, as well as working with X numbers of humans. So let's start with Cubitt. Let's start with. So basically, if we have two cubits. So in the example, both can be in the zero state, both can be in the one state and both can be in different other states. And this can happen in four more ways since there are four different states.

For a system with two qubits, we can model the system as a normalized vector in a vector space of four dimensions. So in other words, in a four dimensional vector space. So also the standard basis of our vector space will have the following Shubert's combination so basically you can see them right here. So since we have two cubits, we will have zero zero zero one one zero and one one. And here we need to understand that a cubit can be in the state zero or at the state one at the same time.

So basically with two cubits, it's possible to have four states like it's written right here. So for now, it's pretty simple, since we are only having a two Cubitt system, but let's say that we have a 50 cubits system, so it's a bit complicated to write down plenty of ones and zeroes. So for each blending of ones and zeros, for each piece is a vector. So a simple way to write down those vectors will be with the use of decimals. So basically, in other words, let's say giving a value to each vector. For example, let's say we have our zero zero right here. This will have the value zero.

One will have value. Zero will have the value two and one. One will have value. So with this, it's possible to convert the binary representation of those cubits into this symbol, so basically there is a formula to do it. There is not really a formula that will simply convert it. And it's then, well, it's way more simpler to work with decimals than to work with the ones and zeros in binary numbers so that working with X number of. So basically when we have two cubits, the thing is we can have four states, but if we have, for example, a random amount of capital, let's say, for example, we have 50 cubits, how can we know exactly the number of states that we can have?

So basically, how many states is it possible to have and how we can define how complex it is to, well, to quantum compute all those states. So it's pretty simple to use the formula below. So basically it's two at power and in the end will simply be the number of cubits. So let's say, for example, we have two cubits. So it's going to be two at power two. And we can have four states similar to each other simultaneously. So basically, at the same time, we can have four states, but now let's say we have 50 cubits.

So in this case, the number of possible states will be two at power 50, which is a pretty trend to Mantus' amount of states that can possibly happen. So basically, this is where you can see the power of quantum computing since, for example, if we only have wealth, since if we're, for example, working with only bits, what's going to happen is that you can only have one state at the time. So basically to have this well, it's possible to have this amount of states in which there are normal bits, but it's going to be one calculation or one state at a time. But in quantum computing, you will have all the states at the same time. So basically it will make all the calculations at the same time, which is pretty cool.

And that can save us plenty of hours of calculation. So something that can take years for a normal computer can take minutes or even seconds for a quantum computer to me. So basically some really advanced versions then for well, another state that is really important to understand, especially in quantum computing. So this type of state is called the uniform superposition, so they said, well, so what is it exactly? Uniform superposition. So it's pretty simple.

It's a state where the probability of collapsing the state vector with any other vector between the bases vectors will be the same. So that is all the basis. Vectors have pretty much the same amplitude. This is why we can call this state a uniform superposition. So basically understand it better. We can take a basic example of about. So let's say that we have, for example, a system with only one Kubic. So the uniform superposition will be the plurality of one half collapsing to the state zero or the state one.

So in this case, with a system with only, well, there is a calculation that can be made that will say that we have zero point five percent well, zero point fifty percent of chance of hitting the zero or 50 percent of chances of hitting the one. So basically, this would be for you in his superposition and it will be pretty much the same thing for what we can calculate it for a higher number of Cuba. So basically, this is just an example of one Cuba. But you can do the same thing with pretty much what we can do the same thing with a lot of other Cubans.

Basically, we can do it with two, three, four or an infinite number of Cubans. And this is exactly where it's important to transform your numbers. Well, you're well, your crewmates, your binary numbers into decimal. So basically, this is where the utility of the transformations of binary into the smallest of basically zeros and ones into decimals will be really important to make to the vectors that you are going to work with. So right now, you guys understand a little bit more what exactly is a but once again, my goal here is not to give you all the mathematical demonstrations, because once again, I don't want you to be a professional in this field.

It's just an introduction for you guys. So I hope you understand the basic mathematics behind until now. And as you can see, it's something that is really, really useful, especially in quantum computing. Well, it's the place where it's used the most. While quantum computing can't really be possible without the Cuban. And basically, as you can see, this is the basic mathematics behind all this. And there is some really advanced mathematics to all this. But this is really the basics who just give you an introduction to all this. So that's a twist. Guys, guys, see our next class.

Introduction To Different Types Of Quantum Computing Algorithms

Hello, guys, and welcome back to the class, Of course, with the complete introduction to quantum computing. So in this class, we are going to talk about another topic that is quantum computing algorithms. So what we're going to view in this part of the Book are the different quantum computing algorithms that can exist. Well, we're going to talk about the different types in the next few classes. I'm going to explain each of those types.

And basically my goal here is really to present you with each type of algorithm. And what are the algorithms that are presented in each of the algorithm types? So you'll see it's well, it's advanced. But once again, my goal here is really to bring you an introduction to different quantum algorithms so you guys can have a basic idea of what those algorithms are. So let's start. All right.

So the first thing that we need to do would be defining what is a quantum algorithm and not even defining what a quantum algorithm is, but simply defining what an algorithm in general is, because not everybody basically knows what an algorithm is. So basically, when we're talking about an algorithm, we can say that it's simply a step by step procedure to be able to execute an operation that can be, for example, a basic mathematical calculation or a construction that can be put in sequences to resolve to resolve a certain problem with the use of a computer.

So basically, as I said, it's well, it's instructions. You can say it's like instructions, basically. So the algorithm will respect certain instructions to be able to resolve a certain problem or to be able to resolve a, let's say, a calculation, for example. Now I want to understand basically what exactly the difference is between a normal algorithm and a quantum algorithm. So it's pretty much the same thing.

The only difference is that the problem is solved with the use of a quantum computer. So in normal, a normal algorithmic algorithm works on a normal computer. The quantum computer will work with a will on the quantum computer. So basically quantum algorithms work with quantum computers and cannot be run on a normal computer. So in other words, a classical algorithm can still be measured on a quantum computer.

But too well, basically it can work in a classical problem, and can be run on a quantum computer. But the reverse, it's not really possible, but it's well, it's a bit complicated. So basically, in a quantum in a quantum algorithm, what is the main difference in a quantum algorithm? Quantum algorithm? There is at least one step that is quantum. So in other words, this means it will work with the use of superposition or entanglement.

So basically, at least one step of our instructions inside of our algorithm. So there's a situation where, well, a series of steps. So basically in at least one of those steps, we need to have a quantum step. So basically, when we talk about quantum steps, we can talk about, for example, entanglement or superposition.

So if there is no state that is quantum, we can not say that this is a quantum algorithm. It will simply be a classical calculation or a classical algorithm.

Now, what are the different types of quantum algorithms that exist? So basically there are some other types of quantum algorithms that exist, but those, in my opinion, are the most popular. So basically we have well, the first one would be the fully transformed algorithm. And we can say that it's the quantum version of the discrete, discrete, fully transformed. So it's well, it also can be integrated very efficiently and operate well in a quantum computer. So basically, we can integrate it in a quantum computer and it will be very efficient. So, for example, what a few examples of this type of algorithm could be.

For example, in our case, um, the sure or the algorithm, which are the two most popular, fully transformed algorithms. And the algorithm is pretty popular in quantum computing in general. The next step of algorithms that exists will be the amplitude amplification algorithm. So this type of algo works with a circuit. What works with a certain speed? That is choosing from a quantum space, we can also say that this type of algorithm is a generalization of, in this case, the group algorithm.

So the algorithm, which is once again a part of the amplitude amplification algorithm, so we can have a reverse algorithm and the quantum counting algorithm. Once again, those types of algos, we're going to talk about them a little bit more in depth in the next few classes. So I'll try to explain a little bit the difference between the different types of algorithm.

Next time that we are going to talk about will be quantum algorithms. So what we can say about it is that this type of algorithm is based on the classic random Wolke algo. So basically, which is a classical algorithm and can be viewed as the quantum version of this algo, we can describe this algorithm as a quantum superposition. You can say it's a superposition over some states. This algorithm can be an expansion. Well, it can exponentially increase the speed of execution of certain problems. So basically what it will do, well, it can for certain problems. Once again, it can really grow the speed of execution. So instead of executing some problems and let's say, I don't know, a few hours, it's going to take you a few seconds, for example.

And finally, we can have the classical algorithm, classical, quantum, classical, quantum algorithms, which can also be hybrid. Well, we can call it a classic hybrid quantum algorithm. So this type of algal algos are a combination of classical optimization and the quantum state measurement. So basically, those will be the four algos that we are going to talk about in the next few classes. And you'll see, yeah, it sounds a little bit complicated, but I'll try to explain it as simply as possible and give you the best introduction possible to this type of. So that's it for those guys.

Quantum Computing Algorithms
Part 1

And welcome back to another class of our Book about the complete introduction to quantum computing. So in this class, we are going to talk about the first type of algorithms to be seen in this part of the Book. We're going to talk about different algorithms that are used in quantum computing, and we are going to start with the fully transformed algorithms. So basically, what I'm going to do is I'm going to present a few algorithms.

I'm not going to make all the mathematical explanations for each algorithm and talk about all the math behind it. And once again, my goal here is really just to give you an introduction to a subject as well as an introduction to algorithms. So let's start. All right. So for the Fwy transform programs, well, basically, the quantum Fwy Transform algorithm can also be seen as a linear transformation. So basically a linear transformation that will work with Kupets. So in other words, it can also be seen as the quantum version of the inverse discrete transform for you.

And this time of this type of quantum algorithms is part of the blending of different algorithms, such as, for example, we can see here the Simon's algorithm or the algorithm that is one of the most popular. So basically it can be performed efficiently. Well, it can be performed efficiently on a quantum computer. So basically the three transfer algorithm is really made for quantum computing. And, well, it's as I said here, it's the quantum version of the universe. This is good for your transformation.

But basically this type of algorithm is really made for quantum computing and can work perfectly when used on a quantum computer. So for algorithms that we are going to talk about today, we are going, first of all, to talk about the sort algorithm so we see what exactly it is. So what we can say about this algorithm, first of all, for the algorithm is that it's a polynomial time or in other words, a time complexity algorithm for the composition of a composite number into a product of smaller integers or in other words, into an integer fact, factorization. So it can, for example, define the prime factor of certain categories. And so let's say we have a of let's say we have an and and what it will do, it can define the prime factor of this number of the number.

And so this is where the algorithm for the seventh algorithm, it's a bit different from first of all, it has been created by Daniel Simons in nineteen ninety nine four. And obviously this algorithm has been extremely useful to solve some kinds of problems and has been created especially to solve the Semmens problem that have been created with well, by assignment's as well. So what exactly is the Semmens problem? So basically the same. Simon's problem is simply a computer computational problem that can be solved way faster with a quantum computer that with a traditional computer.

So basically, this problem is not necessarily, well, let's say something that is complex or really useful in real life, but just a certain problem that can prove that quantum computing works way better. Well, quantum computing is way faster than traditional computing. And basically with the use of the Semmens algorithm, it's possible to solve this problem way faster with this algorithm than to use a traditional computer, for example, as well. So for both of those algorithms, the use of it, well, the use of it can be in, for example, quantum research.

Well, there are places where you can use those algorithms, but it's not like, well, it can be used in real life, but it's usually used in places. For example, in research. It can be used, for example, I don't know, in physics it could be used in mathematics. In engineering, in electricity, so in fields that are really scientific and that requires a lot of mathematics, it's really used a lot in quantum research, especially the Book algorithm, which is really, really popular in this field. And basically this is for now, this is the main goal of them.

So it's really used in that research to be able to build the future of quantum computers. So I hope right now you understand a bit more first what some of the algorithms of well, in quantum computing that we have. So he's a first class guy in our next class.

Quantum Computing Algorithms Part 2

Welcome back to the class of our Book for the complete introduction to quantum computing. So in today's class, we are going to talk about different quantum computing algorithms. And once again, we are going to talk about another type of quantum computing algorithm that is the amplitude amplification algorithm. So basically, we're going to talk about algorithms that are in this type of algo. So let's start. All right.

So basically, what exactly is the amplitude amplification, algorithms or algorithms that are based on amplitude amplification? So basically this algorithm works by allowing the amplification of a certain subspace of a quantum state usually. So usually the application of this algorithm will lead to an exponential increase in the speed of problem solving. If we compare it to other classical algorithms, what I can see here is that it not only leads to exponential speed increase, but it's going to lead to quadratic speed increase.

And finally, also, this type of algorithm is mostly used well, when it's used to describe the Liberty Bell availability, bias or cognitive risks. So basically it's used in, well, not plenty of fields, but usually on a quantum level, it can be used on plenty of fields. And mostly the algorithms that we are going to talk about can be used in cryptography, can be used to account for counting, can be used for problem solving, or it can be used also for statistical purposes. So two algorithms that we are going to talk about today will be the Grover's algorithm, as well as the quantum counting algorithm and basically the Gruver.

Well, the algorithm is a quantum algo that is able to define that unique well, the unique solution to a black box function in all this with very high probability. So basically, the black the black box can be used in plenty of fields. It could be in engineering, in physics, and it could be in mathematics. And basically, it can be applied to pretty much any type of problem that we don't know the inputs to. So also, the algorithm is not only providing exponential growth and speed if it's compared to classical algos, it's providing quadratic speed-up. So as I said in the beginning and in other words, it can be really useful in many things.

So, for example, cryptography sits since it can brute force, really advanced systems and a small amount of time. So in other words, what exactly is brute force? So in the hacking general, not in hacking, but let's say, for example, you want to find a certain password and there is a technique called brute force. So when you are brute force and you will simply test all the possible strategies and what exactly this algorithm can allow you to do is to test all these strategies in a very short amount of time. So let's say, for example, you have a 64 bit system. Well, yes, the 128 bit system. And basically you will have a thousand well, encryption keys or encryption keys.

You will have millions, if not billions of different company possible combinations. And basically this algorithm is able to test all of those combinations in a pretty short amount of time. So basically, by using it, you will be able to not destroy the model in cryptography, but it's going to be a big hit in modern cryptography and modern security. So basically, this is why quantum computing could be a really good thing. But at the same time, some fields such as security can see it as a threat. And with quantum computing, when quantum computing will become more available, the security will definitely need to be upgraded because it will be pretty simple to brute force any password with any quantum computer. All right.

The same algorithm right here will be the quantum counting algorithm. And it's a quantum algorithm that is used to count basically the number of possible solutions that a certain problem can arise. So it's really on a basic level and. It can do it in a really efficient way. So basically, this algorithm is also based on Goober's search algorithm and it's based on the algorithm right here and also in this field, in the field of quantum computing, this algorithm is pretty important since it allows efficient quantum counting.

And finally, this algorithm offers solutions to the quantum existence problem. So basically, this algorithm right here could be really used to, as I said, counting solutions to problems. But what I'm saying is, it's not only a solution, it could be used in really advanced statistics. It could be used, I don't know. Well, usually in probabilities and statistics and with quantum computing, it's possible to basically use the statistics in real terms.

If we want to talk about the modern world and what field of the modern world it could be used. For example, think about high frequency trading. So basically, with quantum computing implemented into high frequency of frequency trading, those businesses will have a really, really big advantage by using quantum computers because it will allow them to make transactions at the second. Even now, they have really advanced technologies. But with quantum computing, it's going to be even bigger.

And this algorithm can do one of those algorithms that are used to basically count probabilities on a certain transaction or on a certain event to cure. So I hope you guys right now understood, understood all the basics of this type of algorithm. So we talked today about amplitude amplification, algorithms or algorithms that are based on amplitude and defecation, the reverse algo, and finally the quantum counting algorithm. So that's a first class guy into our next class.

Quantum Computing Algorithms
Part 3

Hello, guys, and welcome back to another class of our Book about the complete introduction to quantum computing. So in this class, we are still going to talk about quantum computing algorithms and we are going to talk about the quantum walk algorithm. So basically, we are going to talk about this algorithm.

And then after we are not going to talk about different algorithms in this type of algorithm, we are going to talk about a type of problem that this algorithm will actually solve. So you'll see it's pretty interesting. So let's start. Right. So basically, what exactly is the quantum Wolke algorithm? So basically the quantum Wolke algorithm, how we can see it is well, at first it's the quantum version of the classical random walk. So for those who are not sure what a random walk is, it's a mathematical concept that can also be called a random process that is used to describe, let's say, a certain part that contains a certain succession of random steps. So we see the main difference between the classical and the world.

The classical random walk and the quantum random walk is the element that allows the random randomness. So what I'm trying to say is that, basically in quantum walk, randomness can happen by the collapse of the waves. The wave functions, the quantum superposition of states and the non-random with a reversible unitary evolution. So basically. Well, well, another thing. Well, for this. For the first part.

For the same part, basically, the quantum world admits that formulation continues in discrete terms. So basically, it will admit formulation continues in discrete terms. And what do you guys need to understand here? Well, basically, what exactly does this mean? So the two elements right here that are continuous and discrete times are alternative frameworks that are used to model variables that evolve over time. So we say this is for the quantum walk algorithm and a problem that it helps us to solve.

Well, basically, this problem can be solved in different ways, but it can also be solved in a quantum way. So basically, it's called the element distinctness problem. So what exactly is it? So it's also known as the element uniqueness problem. So element distinctness problem is the problem of the determination of the distinction of elements. So in other words, if elements from a certain list are distinct, elements from a certain list are distinct. Yes. Or them. So this type of problem can be solved in many ways. So if we're talking about classical ways that this problem can be solved. So, for example, we can use what we can use, randomize the algorithm or we can use decision trees, for example.

So basically, what exactly is this well, what exactly is broken? So let's say we have a list and we are trying to find those distinctions in this list. And basically this would be the step from so it's possible to also solve this problem. In a quantic, we end up with the use of the quantum work algorithm. It's possible to solve it. So basically there are other algorithms that can solve this type of problem. But basically what's cool with solving it with the quantum algorithms is that, first of all, it will take way less time. And second of all, there are plenty of other advantages. But the most important one is that it takes less time. So time is a really important factor and it also requires less variables and less Kettlewell, less calculations. And the calculation time or process will be less, not less complicated, but less heavy.

We can say it this way than the use of classical models, for example, classical algorithms or other classical ways to solve this type of problem. So I hope you guys understand what exactly is the quantum world and what type of problem it helps us solve in this case. So that's it for us. Thanks, guys. In our next class, where we are going to start to talk about Microsoft Cube and other different tools that you can use to be able to, well, to work with quantum computing.

Introduction to Microsoft Q#

Hello and welcome back to our class of our Book about the complete introduction to quantum computing. So in this part of the Book we are going to talk about in this part of the Book, we are going to talk about more about the program, National Park and what we are going to talk about.

Well, what programming language we are going to use, we are going to use cute language. So basically, this is a programming language to have been developed, developed by Microsoft. And basically we are going to work with it to be able to perform different operations. So once again, my goal here is just to give you an introduction to this programming language, as well as the notebook that we are going to use to be able to perform everything. So let's start. All right.

So basically, what exactly is Microsoft? So Microsoft is an open source programming language, so in other words, it's especially used to develop as well as running different quantum algorithms. Also, this programming language is part of the Kudi, Kate, or in other words, the quantum development kit. So when we're talking about this kit, well, this kit includes plenty of interesting elements, such as, for example, the quantum, small quantum.

Some leaders, IP, API Documentation's CU libraries were even extensions for other programming environments. So it also not only includes elements that I just mentioned, the quantum development kit has other types of libraries, such as machine learning libraries, medical libraries or even chemistry libraries. So this programming language is pretty advanced indeed. It's sports, a basic procedural model to write different statements. Come on, come on. Data types and loops with Python as well as C, so basically you can work with other programming languages.

It also has quantum operations as well as quantum specific data structure. So basically this well, not this program, this programming language and the tricky word quantum development kit are all based around that well, creating quantum algorithms and working with different quantum algorithms. So basically you can use it for this purpose. It has everything you need to be able to use it for this purpose. And also you can use it with multiple different other programming languages.

So basically, there are tools that will allow you to work with different programming languages as well. So basically, if you have an application, another programming language, it's possible to merge them together. So this is pretty cool with the Microsoft Cube, the programming language. Right. What exactly can you do with the Kuriki or the quantum development kit? So basically you have the possibility to develop in current environments and common tools. So what does this mean?

So as I said, it's possible to integrate quantum development with different programs such as, for example, we can think about visuals to you. It was a very popular notebook. So for programmers, this is pretty popular. Also, it's possible to pair the created programs with other languages, such as, for example, Python. So this would be the most popular programming, language oriented, also done that, for example, for others. So it allows us to work with different worlds, with different quantum operations.

So once again, the quantum development kit offers the possibility to test different quantum algorithms. So. All this, while testing those operations, will allow us to explore different concepts, quantum concepts such as, for example, entanglement or the superposition as well as other quantum operations. So there are plenty of others and you can all test them with this quantum development kit. So the different libraries that the queue language contains allow the possibility to run advanced quantum operations without necessarily having to create some basic operations.

What you need to do with other programming languages. And finally, allowing us to create quantum programs will allow us to do quantum programs simulation so it offers up when you create a quantum program, basically you want to simulate it or you want to run it. And what it does, it allows where it gives a full state quantum simulation. You can simulate it as well in a limited scope to fully simulate or then use other resources to test your Q programming language code with different resource estimates.

So basically the cue to programming language is really a language that is used for quantum programming. Once again, this is an advanced level programming language and once again we will see what we'll do in the next few classes. We're going to learn the basics of it. So basically, you learn to do some basic operations and you'll see it's pretty cool. So if you have some python, some programming experience, not only in Python, but in any other programming language, you'll see it's not that complicated to understand.

But what's cool about it is that you can run some quantum operations once again. You will not be a professional in your programming language by the end of this class, but at least you will have the perfect basics to be able to start in this field. So it's the first class that goes into our next class.

Setting Up Everything

Oh, yes, and welcome back to another class of our Book about the complete introduction to quantum computing. So in today's class, we are going to set up all the tools that we need to be able to work with Microsoft. And basically what we need to do is download a code editor and the editor that we are going to use to work with Microsoft is pretty simple.

It's called Visual Studio Code. So how exactly do we download this code? Well, it's pretty simple. First thing that you guys will need to do is simply let's say you are on Google. What you want to do is download visual studio code. So basically you simply write down visual studio code and you should have access to it. So the logo looks something like this. It's pretty simple. It's going to be the first thing right here. Simply click on it and then you can click on the download button.

So basically you just need to choose your type of my windows. And from the point that you have downloaded Visual Studio, you can download the different plugins. So for example, you can download Python. So you have access to Python, you have access to different programming languages and you can all download them to be able to work with them. So personally, I have Python in my visual studio code. If you work with Python, you can download it as well. If not, well, it's not a big deal. All right.

So the next thing that we need is downloading Microsoft. So basically, if we want to have access to Microsoft, you well, we need to download it as well. So pretty simple. What I do is I simply write down on Google, Microsoft, one time development kit, visual studio, and it's going to be the one right here. So pretty simple. Simply clicking on the install button is really important. If you simply install this well, the development kit, it's not going to work because you don't have a visual studio. So it's really important to download Visual Studio first and then you can download Microsoft Quantum Development Kit.

So if we look at the visual studio, it looks something like this, and here you can find the programs that you have well, not the programs, but the programming languages that you have. So for me, for example, I have Python right here and I have Microsoft Quantum Development Kit that is right here. And from this moment, it's pretty simple. Well, now you have everything you need and you are all set and ready to start. So it's the first class for the guys to open our next class.

Basic Microsoft Q# Operations Part 1

And welcome back to our class, Of course, about the complete introduction to quantum computing. So in this class, we are going to have an introduction to Microsoft Cube, which is the programming language for quantum computing. And what we will do today is pretty simple. We are going to write down a simple line of code that will allow us to test everything and to see that all the downloads that you guys have made are correct and that you are good to go.

So what you need to be able to perform this Book in the next few classes is pretty simple. So you need First Visual Studio, which is our code editor in this case, then you need the EMCDDA, which is right here, Microsoft Development Kit. So Cucu, these include Kayseri, which would be the Microsoft development kit. And finally, the last thing that you guys will need is a dot net. So basically, I'll show you what it is exactly. So it's a framework and you need to be able to run the apps that we are going to create. So pretty simple.

Simply write down that net on Google and you should be redirected on a Microsoft page. It looks something like this and you simply can download the version right here. So basically the most basic version, if you want to build up apps, apps, it's going to be this one right here. All right. So when you have everything downloaded and everything is ready and good to go, doing it right now is pretty simple. We can start creating our project. So basically what we'll do at first is pretty simple.

We are going to go on our menu and open up the common palate, so basically right here we are going to open up our command palate from this moment.

What we want to do is to create a new project for our well, for our cook. So we'll see. What we'll do right now is, for example, in Python, you will run your first line of code, which will be Helliwell. So you'll print Hello World. And what we'll do right now is pretty much the same thing. Simply, instead of the world, it's going to be a quantum world. So pretty simple, we are going to create a new project, so simply write down, create a new project. So basically you write it down, you come back here. So it's going to be the one right here. Since I already used it, I simply wrote it down. So cute. And you create a new project.

All right, so when it's done, you need to select the standalone console console application, which is pretty important. So let's call it Quantum Hello one since I already have quantum. Hello. And we are going to create the project when it's done. It's pretty simple. What we'll do right now is we will open the new project page. And here we go, so basically, you guys should have two things right here, so you should have a program called QE and Quantum Hello. One. So we can just click on X on those things. So pretty simple when all this is done.

The next thing that you want to do. Simply go here. So basically we'll just look at what our coats look like. Obviously, as you can see right here, we have our quantum yellow one. And you should have those basic lines of code right here. And you should have another. You should have some other lines of code right there. So basically the file. Well, the first file will define the project settings and will contain basic Q Kyouko. So basically the one right here and the message will be right there. So basically, hello, quantum world, as I said. All right. So the next thing that we want to do is pretty simple.

We want to run everything. So how exactly we are going to run everything. It's pretty simple. Just go to our terminal right here and we are going to generate a terminal. So we are going to have a terminal right here. And then we are going to run everything so exactly do run everything. Pretty simple. We just write down dot net run and click on and then it's going to take a little bit of time. And what we are going to create right now, what we are going to generate in our terminal is pretty simple. We are going to generate this text right there.

Once again, there is no entanglement or any other quantum code, right? It's just a simple code. But once again, it's written in a cute programming language. So as you can see, it has generated a right there. So basically right now we know that everything is set up and everything works fine and you will be able to continue to perform well. You will be able to continue to perform other calculations or write down your code in Q programming language. So right now we have verified everything and we can start using visuals to decode. And at the same time, you already wrote down your first lines of code in Microsoft. So that's at first glance, guys, and see all in our next class.

Basic Microsoft Q# Operations Part 2

Hello and welcome back to another class of our Book, but the complete introduction to quantum computing. So in the best class we have written this, those basic lines of code. And basically our goal was simply to get an introduction to Microsoft and just write some basic lines of code.

But I think it's also important to understand what we have just written. And this is exactly what we are going to do in this class, talking about each part of this little code that we have written in the past class. So this way, you guys will understand the logic behind the new programming language. All right. So basically, how does code start? So our code starts with a namespace. So basically this element of the code is usually used.

Well, it usually uses the two related functionalities and normally every CU file starts with this. Basically, it starts with a namespace and they become pretty important when you have different Q libraries or you write your own library. So basically if you work with other libraries like here, for example, or if you have if you write your own library. Right. Next thing that we are going to talk about. So right now we have our namespace that is called Quantum Hillal, and then we have our libraries right here. So before we start reading or writing our code, which is right there, we import our libraries. But we also need to understand what exactly a library is. So we think programming a language like in other programming languages, such as, for example, Python libraries, is very important. So what exactly is a library?

So it's important, but what exactly is it? So it's a package that contains operations as well as functionalities that can be used in future quantum programs. So it's in quantum computing, but basically it's basically the same thing in Python. So is this: some libraries will give you access to more operations. So, for example, in Python, you have McGlothlin, which is a library in Python. Here, for example, we have two libraries that we are going to use. We use Microsoft, Quantum Chenin, Microsoft Quantum Intrinsic. So there are plenty of standard libraries that exist with Microsoft.

You can, for example, think of Microsoft Quantum Chemistry Library, which is another library that allows the execution of quantum operations related to chemistry.

So basically, this is one of plenty of others. Quantum Leber's. So the library works in a code that 's pretty simple, so first the library is called to get access to all the operations that it contains, then we write the specific operation that we want to use. So, for example, right here we have our message. But another way that we could have written, how we could have written this code would be like this. So I'll just write it down. But in this case, message. So this could be a way to write down our code right here. So just a mistake.

Once again, you can write it this way. So basically, you use your library and then you write down your message. So this could be another way to use our library, which is once again the goal of a library. So basically, first of all, you import your library. What we did right here, we have it for our libraries first and then you write the operation that you want to work with. Also, we are going to usually use that directive to make the code easier to read and understand. So basically, instead of writing down in front of each operation or in front of each function, the library, we just import the library one.

So in this case, we import Microsoft quantum instinct and intrinsic ones and we can use the operations that are related to this library over the whole well when we are writing down our program. All right. Next thing would be the operation. So here we have our entry point, which would be the start of our coding path. So we have our namespace right here. We have the libraries that we have just imported and here we will start to write down our code. So basically, what exactly is an operation? So if you write down the operation, but the operation is basically the foundation of the Kukreja program.

Well, of a program. So in other words, the provision in the programming language is simply a quantum subroutine. So in other words, we can also say that it's a routine that can be called and that has quantum operations that can change the state of the Cubitt register. So let's look at the example below. So here the operation is to say hello. So basically this operation has zero arguments that are telecommuted and will return a unit. So in other words, it just returns a message without information. So basically, here we have our operation, in which they say hello, as you can see right there. Here we have basically what this means.

It means that it will return new information. And the only thing that will return, it will return the message that we ask him to return. So basically, in this case, we asked him to return Helo one, and this is exactly what it does. It returns this little line of code right here. So right now, you understand the basics of this basic line of code. So once again, it's not that complicated to understand. But if you guys want to get better, if you want to understand a little bit better, it's like any other programming languages. It's with practice. So he's a first class guy in our next class.

Conclusion

Hello, guys, and welcome back to the last class of our Book about the complete introduction to quantum computing. So we talked about many, many things in disBook and basically until now, you guys should have a basic understanding of what exactly is quantum computing. So what I want to do right now is pretty simple.

Just want to do a quick summary and talk about basically what's next and what you can do with all this knowledge that you have in this Book. We talked about plenty of things. So first of all, we talked about all the mathematical concepts. So we talked about linear algebra. We talked about quantum superposition, quantum entanglement.

We talked also about what exactly a cubit is, how it works and different Cubitt calculations. And we also talked about algorithms. So basically different quantum algorithms as well. So I explained how each of those algorithms work. And finally, we talked about Microsoft Cube and we did some exercises with Microsoft, which is the programming language for quantum computing. So if you guys are at this stage of the Book, I'm pretty sure that you have completed the whole Book. So I just hope that you guys have liked this Book once again here.

My goal was to make an introduction to the topic. I didn't want to go too much in depth, but once again, my goal here was simply to introduce you to this topic. I'm not going to lie if you guys want to go in depth on this topic, it's not easy. Each of the concepts that I covered in five minutes can take hours and hours and hours to understand properly and to be able to work with. So once again, right now, you have an introduction and you know pretty much what exactly is quantum computing where quantum computing is at right now in the world. And basically, this was the goal of this Book I'm in right now.

What's next? So basically, if you guys really liked and enjoyed quantum computing or a disBook about quantum computing, you like the topic and stuff. So the next thing for you guys would be taking a more advanced quantum computing Book. So if you want to just learn by yourself, dear. Well, there are not that many resources that exist. That's the problem, because this topic is not very, very known. And this is a pretty new topic that is right now that comes right now. And that's pretty much a problem. So it's pretty hard to learn more advanced quantum computing things, but some universities offer interest in quantum computing Books.

So if you or someone who likes to learn just for the purpose of learning, there are some universities that offer this topic. Also, there is a lot of research that is done in quantum computing and in the programming field, you can learn more about Microsoft, which is an amazing programming language, especially if you guys want to continue with quantum computing.

Besides that, I'd like to thank you all for taking this class once again. I was really happy to be your teacher for the past few hours. The Book was probably complicated for you guys to understand. But for me, it was also complicated because once again, as I said, this topic is pretty complicated. And to explain it as easily as possible, to explain the concept that takes hours, to understand in ten minutes, it's not always easy, but I did it and I'm pretty proud of it.

And I hope that you guys liked the way that it was presented and that you guys have it by the end of this Book, learn something new. So if you want to check out my other Books than you like my style of teaching, I have a few of them that are right now online so you can check them out. They're all pretty interesting about different topics besides that. Thanks again for being part of this amazing adventure. And I hope to see you in another of my classes.